EXPLORE
my world

Honey Bees

Jill Esbaum

NATIONAL
GEOGRAPHIC
KiDS

WASHINGTON, D.C.

Look, a honey bee!

Buzzing through a warm afternoon, a little worker bee dips into colorful flowers again ... and again ... and again.

A honey bee visits hundreds of flowers a day, tasting each one with its feet!

From each flower, she collects a sweet liquid called nectar.

She sips the runny nectar through her straw-like tongue and stores it in a special, just-for-honey tummy.

The tongue is called a proboscis (pro-bohs-kis).

Flower pollen dusts the bee like fluffy golden snow.

Every once in a while she stops, rolls the pollen into balls, and stuffs these into tiny sacs on her back legs.

Honey, I'm home!

When the bee is so heavy with nectar and pollen she can barely fly, she heads home to the hive.

Thousands of other workers are arriving home, too.

Inside the hive, the air hums with excitement. Bees bustle to and fro.

The whole colony
works together for
its queen. As long as
she is safe and healthy, so
is the hive.

Worker bees bring her
food and carry out
her waste. They
fan their wings to
keep the hive cool.

A hive is made up of many honeycombs!

One of the most important jobs in the hive is caring for the queen's many eggs.

honey bee egg

Through spring and summer, she lays up to 2,000 eggs per day. She wiggles her abdomen down into a honeycomb and drops each egg into its own six-walled cell.

larva

An egg's shell melts away, and ... hello, larva!

The chubby baby looks nothing like a bee. Yet.

16

For three days, the larva is fed a milky mush called royal jelly. Then it is switched to a honey-pollen mixture called bee bread.

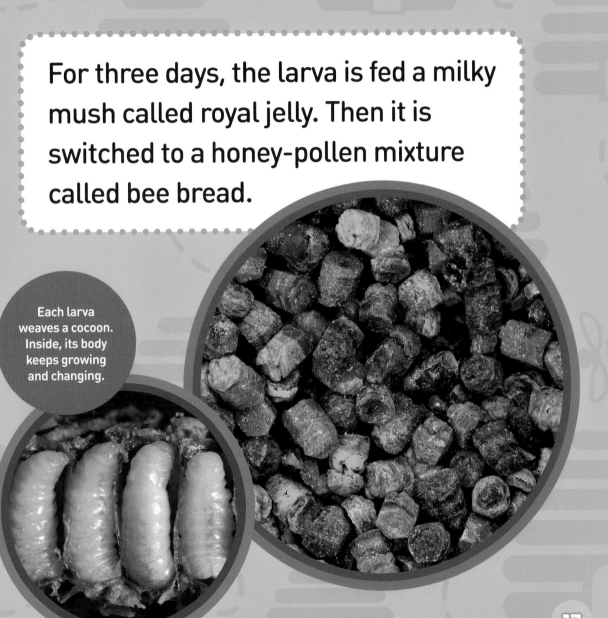

Each larva weaves a cocoon. Inside, its body keeps growing and changing.

Hives can be found in unusual places.

Many honey bees live in human-made hives. A beekeeper opens a hive to remove part of the sticky golden honey. Yum!

Bye-bye, buzzy!

Hope you find a lot of lovely flowers!

Busy as a Bee!

There is plenty of work to do in a honey bee hive. Every worker does each of these jobs in order, moving from one to the next every few days during her six weeks of life.

Worker bees are always female.

1 Clean out cells

Each hive has only one queen bee. She is the only one able to lay eggs. The eggs are as tiny as the very tip of a brand-new crayon.

2 Feed the queen and larvae

Can you buzz like a bee?

What is one chore you do at home?

3 **Build and repair honeycombs**

4 **Make honey from nectar**

5 **Guard the hive entrance**

6 **Fly out to collect nectar**

Have you ever seen a bee on a flower?

Male honey bees, called drones, do not work in the hive and only live long enough to mate with the queen. When fall arrives and the weather turns cold, drones are kicked out of the hive!

Do flowers grow near your home or school?

More Honey, Please!

Bees make honey from flower nectar. They store it in the topmost cells of their honeycomb. They eat both honey and pollen.

Pollen is stored in cells below the honey.

Where do you store your food?

In one day, a worker bee brings home enough nectar to make only a tiny bit of honey. But a hive might have 50,000 or more bees. Working together, they can make as much as two pounds (1 kg) of honey per day. That's enough honey to fill two canning jars.

Pollen cells are built above those filled with eggs and growing larvae.

Do you weigh more or less than two pounds (1 kg)?

What's your favorite sweet treat?

The Bee Is the Key

Do you have a garden?

When bees fly from flower to flower, tiny grains of pollen stick to their feet, then get dropped off on another flower. That's called pollination, and it's what helps flowers make more flowers. Bees pollinate many food crops, too.

salvia plant

Without bees, we couldn't enjoy things like apples, blueberries, cherries, cucumbers, strawberries, or melons.

Have you ever picked apples from a tree?

Bees are important to many ecosystems. You can help them by planting nectar-rich flowers like daisies and marigolds, and blue flowers like salvia. Bees seem to like the color blue! You might also plant any of the fruits or berries mentioned above, as well as broccoli, pumpkins, and tomatoes.

What's your favorite vegetable?

Bee Maze

Help the honey bee find its way
back to the hive!

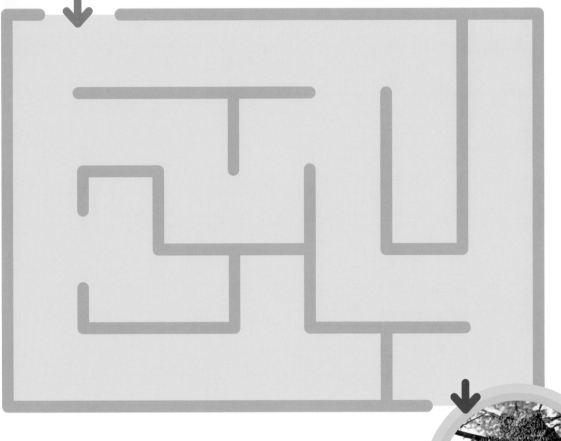

Waggle Dance

When a worker bee returns to the hive, it sometimes does a waggle dance. The special wiggle-waggle moves are actually directions that show other workers where to go to find flowers! Can you look at the picture and waggle dance like a honey bee?

For Hugo and Fiona
—JE

We chose to spell "honey bee" as two words to respect the scientific community's preference. For spelling bee purposes, please note that Merriam-Webster's dictionary spells it as one word, "honeybee."

Since 1888, the National Geographic Society has funded more than 12,000 research, exploration, and preservation projects around the world. The Society receives funds from National Geographic Partners, LLC, funded in part by your purchase. A portion of the proceeds from this book supports this vital work. To learn more, visit www.natgeo.com/info.

NATIONAL GEOGRAPHIC and Yellow Border Design are trademarks of the National Geographic Society, used under license.

Trade paperback ISBN: 978-1-4263-2713-1
Reinforced library binding ISBN: 978-1-4263-2714-8

The publisher gratefully acknowledges bee educator and beekeeper Louise Edsall for her expert review of the book.

Art director and designer: Sanjida Rashid

Printed in the United States of America
22/WOR/6